TIME TRAVEL

Rosen
YA™
New York

CORONA BREZINA

Published in 2019 by The Rosen Publishing Group, Inc.

29 East 21st Street, New York, NY 10010

First Edition

Library of Congress Cataloging-in-Publication Data

Names: Brezina, Corona, author.

Title: Time travel / Corona Brezina.

Description: New York: Rosen Publishing, 2019 | Series: Sci-fi or STEM? | Includes bibliographical references and index. | Audience: Grades 7–12.

Identifiers: LCCN 2017050761| ISBN 9781508180463 (library bound) | ISBN 9781508180470 (pbk.)

Subjects: LCSH: Space and time—Juvenile literature. | Time travel—Juvenile literature. | Time—Juvenile literature.

Classification: LCC QC173.59.S65 B74 2019 | DDC 530.11—dc23

LC record available at https://lccn.loc.gov/2017050761

Manufactured in the United States of America

CONTENTS

Introduction 4

CHAPTER 1
Taking Trips Through Time 7

CHAPTER 2
Problems, Paradoxes, and Ethics of Time Travel 19

CHAPTER 3
Exploring Einstein's Space-Time 29

CHAPTER 4
The Next Frontiers of Time 41

Timeline 53
Glossary 54
For More Information 56
For Further Reading 58
Bibliography 59
Index 61

In 2005, students at the Massachusetts Institute of Technology (MIT) hosted a time traveler convention. They invited time travelers from all eras to visit as many times as they wanted. No confirmed time travelers attended.

If a convention were organized for fictional time travelers, however, organizers would need a huge venue for attendees. Scientists may doubt that time travel is possible, but writers and creators of media such as movies, TV shows, and video games have enthusiastically incorporated time travel into their works. A fictional time travel convention might host superstars such as H. G. Wells's Time Traveler from the novel *The Time Machine* (1895), the Terminator from the 1984 movie *The Terminator*, Marty McFly from the 1985 movie *Back to the Future*, and the Doctor, who has been traveling through time in his TARDIS (Time and Relative Dimensions in Space) since the British TV series *Doctor Who* began airing in 1963.

Time travel is one of many topics in science fiction (sci-fi) that draws the interest of experts in the fields of science, technology, engineering, and mathematics (STEM) as well as the general public. Advances in science and technology are turning some of

Many different forms of media have tackled time travel. Here, a time traveler prepares to depart in the 1960 movie *The Time Machine*, based on the 1895 novel by H. G. Wells.

the classic subjects of sci-fi, such as genetic engineering and robotics, into reality. For more speculative enterprises, such as reviving extinct species, colonizing planets, or cloning human beings, scientists have developed broad scenarios about how to achieve them.

Most scientists, however, do not believe that it is possible to create a time machine that could transport human beings into the past or future. The topic of time is still highly relevant to at least half of the STEM categories. These include scientists such as physicists, cosmologists, and mathematicians working with the complex mathematics involved in understanding the nature of time. Some engineers and technologists may participate in experiments dealing with the physics of time, but they're not yet needed to build and maintain time machines.

Nonetheless, the concept of time travel continues to inspire scientific investigation and creative interpretation. Sometimes, science fiction and scientific breakthroughs even intersect. A 2017 research paper was entitled "Traversable Acausal Retrograde Domain in Space-time" (TARDIS). The mathematicians claimed that time travel was mathematically possible, although the solution utilized exotic matter capable of bending space-time in impossible ways.

If time travel is theoretically possible, why did the time travelers skip the 2005 MIT convention? Perhaps time travelers are very careful to avoid attention. Maybe time travel is just too dangerous or expensive for very many time travelers to take part. It's possible that people of the far future aren't interested in visiting the past, or that they are limited to traveling close to their own timelines. Perhaps regulations restrict time travel to avoid disrupting history.

Of course, there is the chance that time travel is indeed impossible and that time travelers do not exist. But the creators of countless works of time travel fiction have yet to be convinced.

CHAPTER 1

TAKING TRIPS THROUGH TIME

What would happen if a person were transported out of his or her own time and into the past or future? Many classic works of literature, going back a couple of hundred years, have addressed that very question. In Washington Irving's short story "Rip Van Winkle" (published in *The Sketch Book of Geoffrey Crayon, Gent* [1819–1820]), the title character goes to sleep and wakes twenty years later in a world where he has been mostly forgotten. To Rip, it feels like he was transported into the future. Charles Dickens's 1843 novella *A Christmas Carol* introduces ghosts who show the disagreeable Ebenezer Scrooge visions from his past, present, and future. The experience prompts Scrooge to undergo a change of heart, and the book's ending implies that the bleak future scenario that he viewed will not take place. In Mark Twain's 1889 novel *A Connecticut Yankee in King Arthur's Court*, American mechanic Hank Morgan wakes up in medieval England after receiving a blow to the head. He sets about using his technological expertise to transform what he views as a primitive society. He also attempts, with less success, to introduce principles of democracy to a land ruled by a king.

In all of these cases, however, the character is moved through time as a result of mysterious means beyond human control. The term "time traveler" did not even enter the English language until 1895, the year that British author H. G. Wells published *The Time Machine*. The book was a milestone that set many precedents for future writers tackling the topic of time travel. Finally, science fiction characters were charting their own courses through time.

The disembodied form of Ebenezer Scrooge, played by Alastair Sim (*left*) in *A Christmas Carol* (1951), views a grim scene with the Spirit of Christmas Present as he travels through time visiting Christmases of the past, present, and future.

THE ORIGINAL TIME MACHINE

When *The Time Machine* opens, the unnamed Time Traveler has not yet finalized his time machine. He demonstrates a small model machine to his friends, who observe that pressing a lever causes the gizmo to vanish. A week later, the Time Traveler arrives late to a dinner gathering, disheveled and ravenous. He then relates the tale of how he successfully tested the time machine, traveling far into the future.

After activating the time machine, the Time Traveler tells them, he found himself in London in the year 802,701 CE. He soon encountered people who belonged to a society called the Eloi, who were small, delicate, and childlike. They led carefree lives in a decaying city and showed little intellectual curiosity. The Time Traveler, who had been expecting to find an advanced civilization, was disappointed and prepared to depart. But he discovered that his time machine had been stolen.

Eventually, he learned that the machine had been taken by the Morlocks, a primitive society that lived underground. These were apelike people who performed the labor that sustained the Eloi's easy existence, but the Morlocks also survived by killing and eating the Eloi. The Time Traveler succeeded in finding his time machine and, in the midst of a fight with the Morlocks, escaped into the future. This time, he traveled forward millions of years to watch the death of the planet before returning to his own time, where he had only been gone a few hours.

The Time Traveler's friends are skeptical of his story, but he shows them a couple of unfamiliar flowers that he had been given

METRO·GOLDWYN·MAYER presents
A GEORGE PAL PRODUCTION

H.G. WELLS' THE TIME MACHINE

in futuristic METROCOLOR

YOU WILL *ORBIT* INTO THE FANTASTIC FUTURE!

STARRING
ROD TAYLOR
ALAN YOUNG · YVETTE MIMIEUX
SEBASTIAN CABOT · TOM HELMORE

H. G. Wells's *The Time Machine* inspired multiple on-screen interpretations, from the classic 1960 movie, which this poster advertised, to a 2008 episode of the TV show *The Big Bang Theory*.

by the Eloi. After most of the guests leave, the Time Traveler departs on another voyage and is never seen again.

Wells is credited with establishing the time travel genre with this book. *The Time Machine* introduced many of the standard elements and assumptions used in subsequent works of the genre. Wells's Time Traveler considers time travel in logical, scientific terms. He begins with the premise that time is a fourth dimension, alongside the three physical dimensions of length, width, and height. He proposes that it is possible for humans to move through time just as they move through physical space.

His machine has controls that can take a traveler into either the past or the future.

As the Time Traveler explains his invention to his friends, Wells addresses some of the objections that readers might raise. Why can't people see the traveler as he passes by them in time? He's moving rapidly, much as a bullet travels too fast to see. Why isn't he stopped by physical objects in the same location as he's traveling through time? The molecules of his body pass "like a vapor" through any such obstacles.

ADVENTURES IN TIME

Today, time travel fiction is no longer a novelty. Most people are familiar with the concept of time travel and don't ever have the experience of reacting to time travel stories from a fresh perspective. In Wells's time, however, time travel was a completely new concept. Many critics lauded the exciting adventure story in the book but dismissed the premise of time travel as outlandish. A few analyzed the logistics of time travel and raised pragmatic objections. Why didn't the Time Traveler age by the same amount that he moves ahead in time? How would Earth's movement, such as rotation and revolution around the sun, affect the Time Traveler's return to the same physical location?

Wells himself didn't believe that time travel was possible, but *The Time Machine* quickly exerted its influence on a branch of fiction that was emerging as its own genre during the early twentieth century. This new category, which came to be known as science fiction, told stories that included speculative elements based on science and technology. Authors seized on time travel as a plot device in their stories and novels. At first, many science fiction works were classified

SCI-FI SOURCES:
H. G. WELLS,
THE TIME MACHINE

"A glittering metallic framework, scarcely larger than a small clock, and very delicately made. There was ivory in it, and some transparent substance …

'You will notice that it looks singularly askew, and that there is an odd twinkling appearance about this bar, as though it was in some way unreal.' [The Time Traveler] pointed to the part with his finger. 'Also here is one little white lever, and here is another.'"

That's how Wells describes a model time machine in *The Time Machine*—the two levers could move the machine into the past or future. The Time Traveler's machine proved a success, as

As envisioned in the 1960 movie, the time machine operated by actor Rod Taylor incorporated blinking colored lights, levers to move forward or backward in time, and a large revolving wheel in the back.

did the novel itself, which provided the foundation for an entirely new subgenre.

H. G. Wells lived in England during a period of tension between the working class and the wealthy upper class. In *The Time Machine,* he refers to the "widening gulf" between classes in his own time, and this notion is reflected in his representation of the far future. Humankind has been divided into two societies—the Eloi and Morlocks—that do not mix:

> So, in the end, above ground you must have the Haves, pursuing pleasure and comfort and beauty, and below ground the Have-nots; the Workers getting continually adapted to the conditions of their labor.

Many authors writing about time travel since have followed Wells's example. In addition to keeping up with the latest breakthroughs in science and technology, they have incorporated contemporary social issues into their time travel scenarios.

as "pulps," published in cheaply produced magazines. The genre grew more sophisticated, however, and earned a wide readership.

Today, numerous sci-fi books and stories of the twentieth century are considered classics of literature, and these include many examples involving time travel. Most of these depart significantly from H. G. Wells's template of a time machine. Some qualify as "hard" sci-fi works that incorporate cutting-edge technology and scientific research, but more often, time travel is used as a convenient plot device or a means of examining contemporary social issues.

In his 1941 story "The Garden of Forking Paths," the Argentine writer Jorge Luis Borges questions the very nature of time. His main character, Dr. Yu Tsun, is a German spy in

England during World War I. As he attempts to transmit some secret information to Germany, he visits a man named Stephen Albert. Coincidentally, Albert had studied the life work of Yu Tsun's ancestor, Ts'ui Pên. He concluded that Ts'ui Pên had envisioned time as not a single path, but an infinite number of possibilities that can split into forks, run parallel to one another, and meet up again. This interpretation prompts the reader to consider Yu Tsun's actions and the events of the story regarding the "forking paths" of time, in which there are many alternate outcomes.

In 1955, the renowned sci-fi writer Isaac Asimov examined how time travel could be used for social control in his novel *The End of Eternity*. It depicts a far future in which the course of history is managed by time-traveling men known as Eternals, who live outside the passage of time. The main character, technician Andrew Harlan, breaks the laws of Eternity by removing a woman from her "hometime" in the five hundred seventy-fifth century. His action sets off a chain of events that threaten to radically alter the past and future.

Kurt Vonnegut's 1969 novel *Slaughterhouse-Five* tells the story of Billy Pilgrim, who experiences the events of his life out of order in time. At one point, he survives the firebombing of Dresden, Germany, during World War II. At another, he is abducted by aliens called the Tralfamadorians. *Slaughterhouse-Five* is a satirical novel, in which Vonnegut uses science fiction elements to examine themes such as war, mortality, and free will.

In Octavia Butler's 1979 novel *Kindred*, an African American woman named Dana is repeatedly pulled back in time to 1815, where she is a slave on a plantation. She realizes that she is being transported to the past to protect the life of the man who will become her ancestor. As a plot device, time travel allows Butler to portray Dana's horror at experiencing the harsh, brutal conditions of the plantation as a contrast to her comfortable life in 1976.

Douglas Adams's *Hitchhiker's Guide to the Galaxy* series of books presents a comedic and often thought-provoking depiction of a universe full of quirky characters and phenomena. Time travel is discussed—in *The Restaurant at the End of the Universe*, published in 1980, Adams addresses the grammatical difficulties created by time travel.

The 1980 novel *Timescape*, by author and astrophysicist Gregory Benford, portrays the working lives of scientists who are attempting to transmit a message backward in time. In the future year of 1998, ecological disasters threaten the planet's future. A group of scientists believe that if they send a warning to researchers back in 1962, the environmental crisis can be averted. But as an indirect result of the communication from the future, the assassination of John F. Kennedy is prevented, causing a paradox that splits the passage of time into two alternate universes.

In Dan Simmons's 1989 novel *Hyperion*, a group of future travelers share their stories with each other. They are all passengers on a spaceship bound to the Time Tombs, structures on the planet Hyperion believed to be traveling backward in time after having been constructed in the far future. All the travelers have had their lives affected by the Shrike, the fearsome time-traveling guardian of the Time Tombs.

Children's books also seize on time travel. Young readers can enjoy adventures through many different periods of history in Lloyd Alexander's 1963 book *Time Cat: The Remarkable Journeys of Jason and Gareth*. Many young adult readers are familiar with Madeleine L'Engle's book *A Wrinkle in Time*, also published in 1963, in which the characters travel through time and space using a phenomenon called a tesseract. The British writer Diana

Earth is destroyed in the opening scenes of the 2005 movie version of *Hitchhiker's Guide to the Galaxy*, in which aliens have mastered time travel and many other sci-fi concepts.

Wynne Jones set her 1987 book *A Tale of Time City* in a city that exists outside of time. J. K. Rowling included time manipulation in *Harry Potter and the Prisoner of Azkaban*, published in 1999, in which Hermione can exist in two places simultaneously by using a magical Time Turner.

As demonstrated by these titles, the time travel genre has evolved over the decades to include many different approaches to the subject in a variety of types of literature. Time travel spread beyond the printed word, as well. Wells's *The Time Machine* was made into a movie in 1960, and today time travel can be found in numerous films, TV shows, cartoons, and video games.

BACKWARD OR FORWARD?

As previously described, time travel offers many different means and directions of travel. Fictional works involving time travel send people into the future and into the past; they may travel minutes, hours, years, centuries, or millions of years. Some involve communication with the past or future rather than physical transport. Time may be described as traveling at different rates in different places or scenarios.

Many important works have followed Wells's lead in exploring the future. Ray Bradbury incorporated an ironic twist in his 1980 time travel story "The Toynbee Convector." Craig Bennett Stiles claimed to have built a time machine and traveled a hundred years into the future. Although people were skeptical of his story, they began to accept his account as human civilization attained a new golden age exactly as he predicted. As an old man, however, Stiles reveals to a reporter that he'd invented the account, believing that human civilization could achieve greatness if people regarded it as their destiny.

Wells's Time Traveler did not venture backward in time, but many other authors have explored the past in their works. An acclaimed example is Connie Willis's *Doomsday Book,* published in 1992, which is set in a future where historians use time travel to study the past. Because of glitches, the young historian Kivrin Engle is stranded in medieval England in 1348 as the Black Plague is raging. In her own year of

In *Groundhog Day*, a weather-man, played by Bill Murray, is inexplicably forced to live his least favorite day of the year over and over again.

2054, her colleagues are battling an influenza epidemic as they seek to bring Kivrin back.

Yet another possibility is the time loop, in which characters relive the same period of time over and over. The best-known time loop occurs in the 1993 movie *Groundhog Day*. A weatherman is inexplicably stuck experiencing the same day again and again as he tries to figure out what he can do to break the cycle.

CHAPTER 2

PROBLEMS, PARADOXES, AND ETHICS OF TIME TRAVEL

One of the most popular time travel adventures is the *Back to the Future* movie series, a trilogy released between 1985 and 1990. The original *Back to the Future* movie describes how Marty McFly, a teenager living in 1985, travels back to the year 1955, the year his parents met in high school. Marty inadvertently prevents his parents from meeting each other for the first time. Worse, his mother meets Marty and develops a crush on him. Marty realizes that if his parents don't become a couple, he will never be born. Therefore, he has to devise a plan to save his parents' relationship and then return safely to the future.

Back to the Future incorporates many of the typical elements found in time travel fiction. To begin, there must be a means of traveling through time and an explanation for how

STEVEN SPIELBERG Presents

BACK TO THE FUTURE

A ROBERT ZEMECKIS Film

He was never in time for his classes...

He wasn't in time for his dinner...

Then one day... he wasn't in his time at all.

In the 1985 movie *Back to the Future*, Marty McFly (played by Michael J. Fox) travels back to 1955, where he introduces his parents' generation to skateboards and rock 'n' roll music. His time machine was a DeLorean automobile.

it came to exist. Marty's time machine is a modified DeLorean car that was invented by "Doc," the mad scientist Dr. Emmett Brown. Most time travel stories introduce complications created by traveling through time, such as Marty's actions altering past events. Finally, there are the ethical considerations of time travel. *Back to the Future* doesn't address this aspect—in fact, Marty's interference in his parents' lives can't be defended as ethical. But plenty of other sci-fi works tackle the ethics of time travel.

BUILDING A TIME MACHINE

In many time travel narratives, a scientist builds a machine that can send a person back or forth in time a set amount and then return that individual to the present. In some scenarios, it's a machine that physically carries the time traveler to another time. H. G. Wells's Time Traveler sits in his machine and monitors the controls as he travels through time, for example, and Marty travels in the DeLorean.

Other time machines send people back without any means of controlling their return. In Willis's *Doomsday Book*, a technician controls the machine by inputting coordinates that send the time traveler into the past. In his 1999 book *Timeline*, Michael Crichton utilizes an experimental machine that sends his characters to alternate universes that are essentially indistinguishable from the past of the real world, creating the effect of traveling through time. The travelers are dependent on the "transit pad" in their home universe to bring them back.

Some high-tech time travel devices are introduced to the present day by travelers from the future or from extraterrestrials. In the 1984 blockbuster movie *The Terminator*, the title character is sent from the year 2029 back to 1984 to change the future by committing an assassination. People being transported into the past arrive in a glowing sphere of energy, although the equipment and methods are never fully explained. Another memorable and chilling example is Lewis Padgett's "Mimsy Were the Borogoves," published in 1943. It begins millions of years in the future with a brief description of an inventor tinkering with a time machine. He tests it by attempting to transport a box of his son's discarded toys back in time. Back in 1942, a young boy discovers the box of toys. After playing with advanced technological devices from the future, the boy and his sister develop an understanding, a form of logic beyond the comprehension of ordinary humans of the time, which causes a crisis in the family. In a more recent movie, *Edge of Tomorrow*, released in 2014, a soldier in the future finds himself stuck in a time loop while fighting an alien invasion. He gained the ability through contact with an alien's blood. The aliens can reset time to achieve a particular outcome, and the soldier can exploit alien time travel capabilities to achieve a victory.

Not all time travel devices are high-tech machines, especially in genres such as fantasy or adventure, in which the mechanics of time travel aren't central to the story. Sometimes, time travel is enabled through a device or amulet such as Hermione's Time Turner in *Harry Potter and the Prisoner of Azkaban*. E. Nesbit created an amulet that allows four siblings to visit a past era in her 1906 children's novel *The Story of the Amulet*. In the 1981 movie *Time Bandits*, a map of spacetime stolen from the Supreme Being functions as a time travel device, and in the TV series *Lost* (2004–2010), an ancient wooden wheel on a mysterious island sometimes transports people through time.

In some scenarios, time travel doesn't require any equipment at all. Time slips are a form of time travel that occur unexpectedly for some unknown reason. Twain's Connecticut Yankee is transported to King Arthur's Court through a time slip. Isaac Asimov transfers a man unexpectedly into the far future through a time slip in his

The characters in the 1981 movie *Time Bandits* navigate time using a stolen map that shows the locations of time portals, which are holes in the fabric of the universe.

1950 novel *Pebble in the Sky*. In Jack Finney's 1970 novel *Time and Again*, advertising artist Si Morley is recruited by government agents to participate in a project in which people travel through time via self-hypnosis. Morley succeeds in taking himself back to nineteenth-century New York City.

PARADOXES AND CONTRADICTIONS

As seen from various time travel scenarios, time travel—especially into the past—has the potential to cause troublesome unintended consequences. Some of these involve paradoxes, in which a proposition leads to a logically unacceptable conclusion even when based on sound premises. One of the most notorious time travel paradoxes is the "grandfather paradox," which proposes that someone travels back in time and kills his or her own grandfather, before he had any children. As a result, the time traveler would not be born. But in that case, he or she would not be alive to travel back in time to commit murder. In *Back to the Future*, Marty must prevent a result similar to the grandfather paradox, although instead of killing his grandfather, he nearly prevents his parents' romance. In general, the grandfather paradox can encompass any case in which time travel alters the past in such a way that it makes the original act of time travel impossible.

A related paradox is a scenario in which someone travels back in time to kill Adolf Hitler and thereby prevent World War II. If the individual succeeds, the goal may be achieved, but as a result, there would be no reason in the revised version of the future for the person to travel back in time.

Another complication of time travel is the "butterfly effect," exemplified by Ray Bradbury's 1952 story "A Sound of Thunder." In the year 2055, a safari company takes big game hunters back in time to kill dinosaurs. The particular dinosaurs had been preselected because they would have died soon anyway. A client named Eckels, however, strays off the path during the hunt. When he returns to 2055, he finds that language and historical events have changed during his absence. He looks down and finds a dead butterfly encrusted in the mud on his boots. Time travel stories utilizing the butterfly effect involve a single small change in the deep past that causes significant unintended consequences for the present.

Another conundrum of time travel fiction is the causal loop, in which a time travel event is its own cause. Robert Heinlein utilizes a causal loop in his 1941 story "By His Bootstraps." As Bob, a

The art of M. C. Escher depicts visual representations of paradoxes. In his woodcut *Day and Night* (1938), black and white geese fly in opposite directions into corresponding light and dark landscapes.

graduate student, is working on his thesis on time travel, a time gate opens up in his room, and he is visited by several time travelers who change the course of his life. As Bob grows older, he realizes that all the visitors had been himself at different ages and that with every visit to the initial Bob, the older versions of himself were setting particular events of his future into motion.

In addition to exploring a causal loop, "By His Bootstraps" includes the complication of multiple selves in the same time and location. Many time travel scenarios, however, forbid a time traveler meeting himself or herself for practical, scientific, and philosophical reasons.

ETHICAL QUALMS

Time travelers set off on their journeys for a variety of reasons. Often, it's out of scientific interest; sometimes, the motivation is personal gain, adventure seeking, or a fascination with a particular era of time.

Sometimes, time travel stories consider the ethics of time travel within the narrative. There's no guarantee that altering a specific event will actually lead to the desired outcome, and plenty of time travel tales involve numerous unintended consequences and collateral damage. Marty McFly is ultimately successful in bringing his parents together in *Back to the Future*, but what about all the other situations he affected as he rampaged through the past?

In books and movies in which time travel to the past is routine, there are sometimes guidelines or regulations aimed at minimizing changes to history. The hunters in Ray Bradbury's "A Sound of Thunder" are directed to stay on the path. In Connie Willis's *Doomsday Book*, the equipment is unable to send time travelers to certain periods in time that are vulnerable to change. Historians are also restricted to visiting eras that are not considered dangerous, as determined by a ranking scale.

Organizations that control time travel may have elaborate structures and rules. The group called Eternity in Asimov's *The End of Eternity* engineers events to achieve the best possible result for history. But a character outside of Eternity disparages their mission. She calls them psychopaths who stifle innovation by editing out disasters and potentially dangerous technological developments.

TIME POLICE AND TIME SOLDIERS

The 1994 movie *Timecop* is set in a version of 1994 in which time travel has become commonplace. Police officer Max Walker signs up to work for the Time Enforcement Commission, the law enforcement branch specializing in crimes involving time travel. Early on in the movie, he prevents a time traveler from changing the history of the 1929 stock market crash. This entertaining movie fits into the "time police" subgenre of time travel science fiction. There are many variations on the theme. The time police may be charged with preventing criminals from altering the past or creating paradoxes. Sometimes time police are required to monitor interactions with alternate versions of history or parallel universes.

As revealed in *The Terminator*, time travel can also be used to gain the advantage during warfare. Both sides use time travel to win battles or manipulate historic events to gain a strategic edge, risking the danger, in some scenarios, that they will become stuck in a causal loop.

Some of the most compelling time travel stories are set into motion when an individual attempts to change history by altering past events. In Gregory Benford's *Timescape*, for example, the scientists decide that it's worth risking time travel paradoxes if communication to the past can prevent an environmental crisis. One of the most acclaimed time travel movies, *Twelve Monkeys*,

In the 1995 movie *Twelve Monkeys*, Cole (played by Bruce Willis) is tasked with obtaining information from the past that will enable future scientists to cure a deadly virus.

released in 1995, involves a time traveler from 2035 sent into the past to learn about the origins of a virus that devastated humanity in 1996.

What types of events would be significant enough to merit trying to prevent them from the future, and who would be qualified to make the judgment? Asimov's *End of Eternity* conveys that it's counterproductive to attempt to eliminate difficult events in history. Benford's *Timescape* and *Twelve Monkeys* both demonstrate that the attempt is likely to prove futile.

CHAPTER 3

EXPLORING EINSTEIN'S SPACE-TIME

Meanwhile, as the genre of time travel science fiction grew, the scientific understanding of the physics of time was also undergoing a revolution. Until the twentieth century, scientists considered time to be moving at a constant rate. The scientist Isaac Newton (1642–1727), sometimes called the father of modern science, held that time and space were absolute. Time could not flow at different rates in different places or circumstances. This premise changed with Albert Einstein's groundbreaking work on the nature of space and time. Einstein determined that time was relative. Einstein's innovative work is the foundation for much of the theoretical speculation about time travel among modern scientists.

THE SPACE-TIME CONTINUUM

Einstein put forth his new ideas about time in his paper on the theory of special relativity, published in 1905. He found

One of history's greatest scientific geniuses, Albert Einstein (1879–1955) questioned accepted scientific conventions of his time and pioneered the theory of relativity. This photograph of Einstein dates from around 1910.

that time is not fixed—it passes at different rates for two observers who are in motion relative to each other. As one of his starting points, Einstein stated that the speed of light was the same in every inertial frame of reference, meaning that the speed of light was constant. This concept departed with the theories on light held by other scientists of his day.

If the speed of light was constant, however, it presented a challenge to the idea of relative motion. Imagine a train with a headlight approaching a station. Three observers each watch the train from a different inertial frame of reference—a woman standing still, a man running toward the train, and a driver moving away in the same direction as the train. The speed of the train relative to each of the observers varies. Yet Einstein's claim about the constancy of the speed of light meant that the speed of light relative to the observers could not vary, even though it was following the same path as the train.

If the speed of light could not change, then the resolution to the conundrum lay in the nature of time. Einstein concluded that the flow of time varied for different inertial frames of reference. In people's everyday experiences, the consequences are not noticeable. But at extremely high speeds approaching the speed of light, relativistic effects result in some unexpected phenomena. For someone traveling at near light speed, a property called time dilation slows the passage of time.

Time dilation has been experimentally proven. A highly accurate clock was flown around the world on an airplane while an identical clock stayed on the ground. When they were later compared, the traveling clock was running slow by a tiny fraction of a second. For that clock, time had run more slowly while it moved on the airplane at a high rate of speed.

Einstein also determined that space is relative, and the traveler will also experience something called length contraction. One consequence of Einstein's theory of special relativity is the idea of the space-time continuum. Much as Wells stated in *The Time Machine*, time cannot be regarded as separate from the three dimensions of space. Rather, a four-dimensional concept of space-time includes time as a dimension alongside the three physical dimensions.

Einstein reached one further conclusion in his theory of special relativity that is highly pertinent to a discussion of time travel. He introduced the idea that mass is relative and stated that it is not possible for an object in motion to achieve the speed of light. In 1992, physicist Alan Lightman wrote *Einstein's Dreams*, a fictionalized account of Einstein's development of the theory of special relativity that describes Einstein's vivid dreams of different conceptions of time.

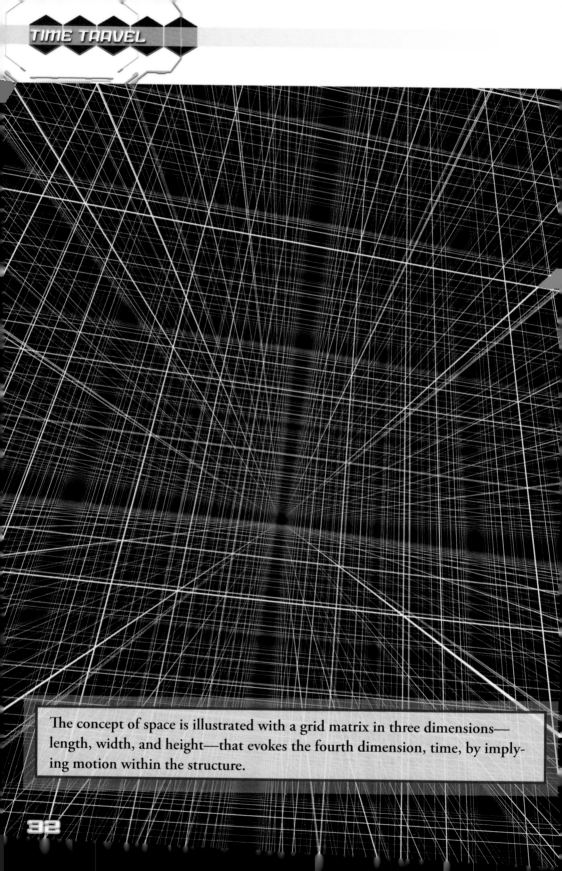

The concept of space is illustrated with a grid matrix in three dimensions—length, width, and height—that evokes the fourth dimension, time, by implying motion within the structure.

BENDING SPACE-TIME

Einstein quickly realized that there were limitations to his theory of special relativity. It applied only to objects moving in a straight line without being affected by acceleration or gravity. In 1918, Einstein released his theory of general relativity, which applied to all motion. Notably for examination of time travel, general relativity accounted for the effect of gravity on space-time. Einstein described gravity as a field. He predicted that light should be affected by the force of gravity and that gravity could also work to bend the very fabric of space-time. Larger objects exert a greater gravitational field than smaller ones. Therefore, a celestial body in space can detectably distort space-time, if only by small amounts. The result is gravitational time dilation, which slows the passage of time.

After Einstein published his theory of general relativity, the mathematician and astrophysicist Karl Schwarzschild applied Einstein's equations to calculate the exact curvature of space-time around a star. He then calculated the geometry of space-time inside a star. Schwarzschild's calculations revealed an odd property of celestial objects. If the body was highly compressed, the calculations for distance, space, and time stopped making sense. Schwarzschild determined the exact size at which any celestial body would exhibit these properties, which depended on the object's mass. Einstein considered such a phenomenon to be purely speculative, with no application in physical reality.

Today, however, it has been proven that these objects, called black holes, exist in space. Most form when a massive star reaches the end of its life and collapses in on itself. The gravitational field around a black hole is so intense that nothing can escape its pull, not even light,

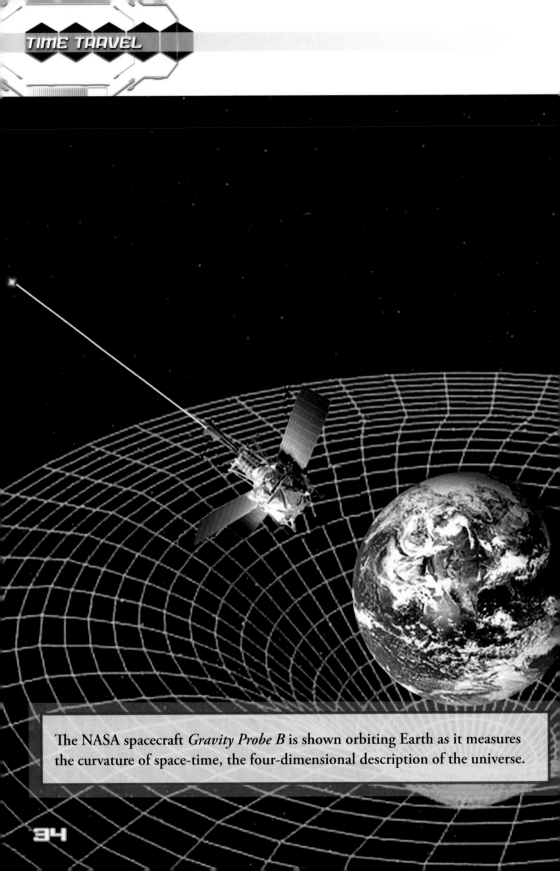

The NASA spacecraft *Gravity Probe B* is shown orbiting Earth as it measures the curvature of space-time, the four-dimensional description of the universe.

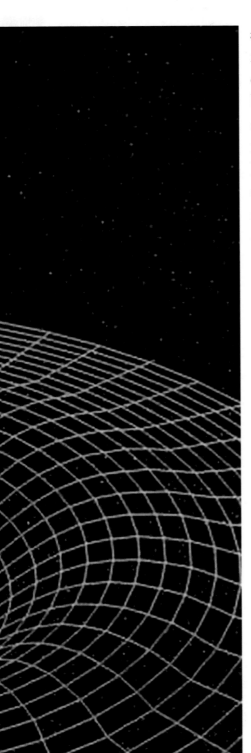

and anything approaching it experiences dramatic gravitational time dilation. The outside limit of the black hole, a sphere surrounding a length called the Schwarzschild radius, is called the event horizon. Inside, matter is concentrated into a small point called a singularity, at which the laws of physics break down. It is impossible to see into a singularity—the interior of the event horizon is isolated from the outside universe.

Sci-fi authors pay attention to scientific breakthroughs involving the nature of time and incorporate cutting-edge concepts into their works. Often, books and movies that involve relativity are hard sci-fi works set in a future in which humans have become spacefarers. Poul Anderson's 1970 novel *Tau Zero*, for example, features a colonization ship bound to a distant planet that accelerates nearly to the speed of light. Because of time dilation, time passes so slowly for the passengers that the universe itself changes significantly over the course of the

WARP DRIVES

Just as scientists and sci-fi writers have speculated about wormholes that could allow faster-than-light travel, they have devised hypothetical machinery that could carry humans through wormholes or use other means to transport people quickly across the vastness of space. One of the best-known such inventions is the warp drive, which has been used in TV shows such as *Star Trek* and *Doctor Who*.

Physicists have proposed theoretical means of manipulating space-time to achieve faster-than-light travel, such as by enclosing a spacecraft in a bubble of warped space-time. The ship is propelled by space-time contracting in front of and expanding behind it. Another mechanism involves sending a spacecraft through a tube of warped space-time connecting two locations in space. Like many proposed means of time

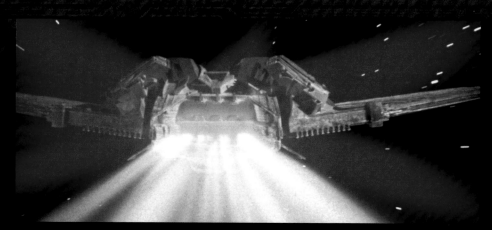

In the 1986 movie *Star Trek IV: The Voyage Home,* Captain Kirk and his crew accelerate at maximum warp speed toward the sun to travel back in time.

travel in physics, theoretical warp drives often require the presence of exotic matter—particles or phases of matter that possess negative-energy-density or other strange properties. Because warp drives involve traveling faster than light, they also suggest the possibility of time travel into the past, which *Star Trek* has incorporated into plotlines.

journey. In Joe Haldeman's *The Forever War*, published in 1974, soldiers are transported vast distances through space at a speed that results in time dilation. Although they are only gone for a few years, decades or even centuries pass on Earth in their absence, resulting in "future shock" at the social changes. Similarly, in the 1968 movie *Planet of the Apes*, a spaceship crash-lands on a hostile planet. Because of time dilation effects, the ship has been traveling for more than two thousand years even though less than two years have passed for the crew.

WORMHOLES AND OTHER SHORTCUTS

Einstein's theories of relativity transformed scientific understanding of the nature of time, but they did not produce a mechanism for time travel. Haldeman's soldiers, for example, experience the passage of time more slowly than the people back on Earth, but they are not transported into the past or future. Yet Einstein's work was so revolutionary that scientists continue to confirm his

predictions and study the rami-
fications of relativity more than
a century later. Physicists and
mathematicians have achieved
new insights regarding time,
including theoretical work on
whether time travel could be
possible.

H. G. Wells's time machine
could transport the Time Traveler to either the future or the past,
depending on the direction of the
lever. According to modern scientists and mathematicians, however, traveling to the future or past
involve completely different types
of theoretical models.

Einstein had a friend, Kurt
Gödel, who was a brilliant mathematician and philosopher. In
1949, he demonstrated that
Einstein's equations for general
relativity allow for the theoretical possibility of closed timelike
curves, or CTCs. He considered a hypothetical universe that
was infinite and rotating. In this
universe, it would be possible to
follow a curving path through
space-time that looped back into
the past. The real universe does

A wormhole can be visualized as the result of folding a flat surface to create a bridge, connecting points that are distant from one another in three-dimensional space.

not resemble Gödel's model, nor did Gödel present it as a realistic possibility. He merely wanted to show that the laws of physics allowed this scenario.

Another theoretical means of time travel was proposed in 1974 by physicist Frank Tipler. The Tipler cylinder is a huge cylinder that is spinning in space fast enough to warp the space-time surrounding it, creating a drag in the direction of its rotation. If people left Earth on a spaceship and were pulled into a warped space-time cylinder's gravitational field, they could emerge into the past or future when they departed, depending on the direction of travel around the cylinder.

The concept of wormholes provides another hypothetical means of traveling through space-time. Imagine a hole punched in the curved fabric of space-time. A wormhole is a shortcut, sometimes described as a tunnel, sometimes as a bridge, that connects distant regions of space on either side of the wormhole. Wormholes also involve the dimension of time—they can be seen as connecting events as well as locations. If someone uses a wormhole to travel a distance of multiple light-years, they will violate special relativity by traveling faster than light. In some scenarios, a wormhole can thereby act as a time machine. Carl Sagan uses a wormhole in his 1985 novel *Contact* as a means of transporting a character to a distant star system. She succeeds in making the trip, but to observers on Earth, it appeared that the machine never left the launchpad. Wormholes have never been observed, however, and gravitational forces would not allow a naturally occurring wormhole to remain open long enough to serve as a shortcut for time travelers.

CHAPTER 4

THE NEXT FRONTIERS OF TIME

Time travel fiction draws on scientific understanding of the nature of time, but the exchange between science fiction and science goes both ways. Many people who work in STEM fields enjoy sci-fi books and movies. Sometimes, the "what if" questions brought up in fiction can even inspire researchers to investigate the scientific and technical implications of the issue in the real world.

An ambitious collaboration between the worlds of science fiction and theoretical physics occurred in 2014 during the production of the movie *Interstellar*. The movie is set in a future threatened by an environmental crisis. Former NASA pilot Joseph Cooper agrees to travel through a wormhole to help discover whether planets many light-years away could provide a new home for humanity. Renowned astrophysicist Kip Thorne acted as scientific consultant to movie director Christopher Nolan, helping create the wormhole as well as other phenomenon such as time dilation near a black hole, a fifth dimension, and the descent beyond the event horizon of a black hole, where Cooper sends a message into the past.

The Cygnus X-1 system, shown in an artist's depiction, is a black hole formed by the collapse of a massive star that is pulling material from a blue companion star.

Following the release of *Interstellar*, scientists such as Neil deGrasse Tyson praised the scientific accuracy of the movie. The process of creating the special effects for the movie even yielded new scientific insights into visualizing a black hole.

THE "ARROW OF TIME"

Whenever a scientist announces a breakthrough or novel insight into theoretical time travel, the news is often greeted with skepticism. Most physicists and mathematicians don't believe that time travel is truly possible. Yet scientists have not been able to provide irrefutable proof of either the possibility or impossibility of time travel. The scientific study of time is a fascinating subject, and debate over the nature of time continues to engage scientists just as it did in Einstein's day.

One of the most enduring arguments against the feasibility of time travel into the past is the "arrow of time." This concept holds that time can travel in only one direction—forward. Many basic laws of physics can theoretically run either backward or forward, but it's difficult to imagine complex physical processes, from forest fires to biological aging to erosion, being reversed. In 1927, the phrase "arrow of time" was first used by astrophysicist Arthur Eddington. He linked the passage of time to the thermodynamic concept of entropy. Thermodynamics is the field of physics dealing with heat and energy, and entropy is often described in simplified terms as a measure of disorder or randomness. Entropy tends to increase over time. According to Eddington, the element of randomness forestalls the possibility of time being reversed.

There are other arrows of time in addition to the thermodynamic arrow of time. The radiative arrow of time is based on the fact that waves, such as light waves and gravity waves, can travel only forward in time. The causal arrow of time deals with cause and effect—a cause must always precede an effect. One event can't occur without the other, and the cause must occur first. The cosmological arrow of time examines the nature of the universe. The universe is expanding, indicating that time is moving in a forward direction outward from an initial small state. Still, none of the arrows of time are accepted as proving without a doubt that time can only flow forward.

According to the "arrow of time" concept, heat from a cup of coffee will be dispersed as it cools, but the opposite process will never occur spontaneously.

As with most scientific topics of time travel, the arrow of time has been referenced in literature. *Time's Arrow*, published in 1991 by the British novelist Martin Amis, is an unconventional narrative rather than a sci-fi novel. It examines the nature of time by telling the story in reverse. Amis begins with the narrator as an elderly man living in the United States and moves backward in time to reveal that he had once been a Nazi doctor committing atrocities during World War II.

THE CUTTING EDGE OF PHYSICS

The twentieth century saw mind-boggling new models and theories in physics, some of which suggested new implications for time travel models. Even as Einstein was putting forth his theories of relativity, other physicists were making discoveries in a new branch of science called quantum physics. While cosmology examines the entire scope of the universe, quantum physics, by contrast, studies particles and phenomena on the subatomic scale. The laws of physics that govern relativity have not been completely reconciled with the laws that govern quantum physics. Nonetheless, quantum physics provides novel tools and concepts for considering the nature of time and the theoretical possibility of time travel.

The properties and behaviors of quantum particles cannot be explained using the classical laws of physics. One such bizarre phenomenon is quantum entanglement, which Einstein described as "spooky action at a distance." Quantum entanglement can be observed between two particles created in a lab at the same time. They remain linked even if they are separated in space. This idea has been tested experimentally by measuring a property of one of the particles. The act of measurement can be observed on the partner particle at the same time, even if the partner has been transmitted hundreds of miles distant from the first. Scientists do not fully understand the physics of this quantum linkage.

Nobody has yet invented a quantum entanglement time machine, but the phenomenon brings up new conundrums in considering the nature of time. Because the particles react simultaneously, the communication between them seems to travel faster than the speed of light, which is impossible according to the theory of relativity. Some scientists have proposed that quantum entanglement acts as an arrow of time. Entangled subatomic particles cause energy to become dispersed, a process that is not reversible.

Quantum physics serves as the basis for the "many-worlds" theory proposed in 1957 by physicist Hugh Everett. Quantum particles often behave randomly according to probability. In the

Time travel could conceivably be possible in a multiverse, in which our own universe is just one of many possible universes that each operate under different laws of physics.

many-worlds scenario, every possible random outcome exists in a series of different universes.

Many other phenomena have been suggested as theoretical means of time travel. Physicists have suggested that a hypothetical particle called a tachyon could travel faster than light. Benford used tachyons for communication with the past in his novel *Timescape*; he also incorporated Everett's many-worlds theory. Another theory proposes that massive "cosmic strings" of energy could stretch across the universe, distorting the space-time around them. The interactions of two such strings could function as a time machine. These are different theoretical strings than those of "string theory" that are hypothesized to make up all subatomic particles—although string theory also allows for a mechanism of time travel.

REIMAGINING TIME TRAVEL

Many books, movies, and TV shows of the twenty-first century have continued to explore the topic of time travel. Like their predecessors, they range from hard science fiction to human interest to social commentary. Audrey Niffenegger's 2003 novel, *The Time Traveler's Wife*, was a hugely popular time travel love story. It tells of the relationship between a woman and her husband afflicted with "Chrono-Impairment." The condition causes him to travel through time uncontrollably and live his life out of sequence.

Robert Charles Wilson's 2005 futuristic novel, *Spin*, tells the story of Jason, a boy growing up in the aftermath of the Big Blackout in which a "spin membrane" enveloped the planet. The barrier dramatically slowed the passage of time on Earth compared to the universe beyond the membrane. Another notable hard science fiction novel was Wesley Chu's *How to Live Safely in a Science Fictional Universe*,

STEPHEN HAWKING ON TIME TRAVEL

Astrophysicist Stephen Hawking is best known as the author of *A Brief History of Time: From the Big Bang to*

The English theoretical physicist Stephen Hawking, known for his work on the origins of the universe and black holes, also writes nonfiction books for nonscientists.

Black Holes (1988). One of the world's leading experts in cutting-edge physics, Hawking does not believe that time travel to the past is possible, although he acknowledges that science has not disproven the possibility. Hawking is, however, a proponent of the many-worlds theory, as he described in a 1999 lecture, "Space and Time Warps":

> According to Quantum Theory, the universe doesn't have just a unique single history.
> Instead, the universe has every single possible history, each with its own probability ... In some histories space-time will be so warped, that objects like rockets will be able to travel into their pasts. But each history is complete and self contained, describing not only the curved space-time, but also the objects in it. So a rocket can not transfer to another alternative history, when it comes round again. It is still in the same history, which has to be self consistent.

Hawking has also suggested a "Chronology Protection Conjecture" whereby the laws of physics act to prevent time travel and the resultant disruption of history.

published in 2010. It tells the story of a time-machine repairman traveling in time around Minor Universe 31 in search of his missing father while his mother lives her retirement in a time loop.

In 2011, Stephen King published *11/22/63*, the title signifying the date that President John F. Kennedy was assassinated. The main character discovers a time portal in a local diner and devises a plan to travel back in time to prevent the assassination. The 2013 literary novel *Life After Life* by the British novelist Kate Atkinson describes the many lives of Ursula, who repeatedly dies, only to have the story loop back to an earlier period of her life and start up again.

Rebecca Stead's 2009 young adult time travel mystery *When You Reach Me* is set in 1970s New York City. After sixth-grade Miranda begins receiving cryptic notes, it gradually becomes clear that they were sent by a time traveler who has come to the past on a specific mission.

The 2004 low-budget movie *Primer* describes how two

Bestselling author Stephen King incorporated time travel into his 2011 novel *11/22/63*, which was adapted into a TV miniseries in 2016.

engineers succeed in building a time machine that can transport people a short distance into the past. Complications ensue in which their time travel alters the future and strains the friends' relationship. Woody Allen's 2011 movie *Midnight in Paris* depicts a time-traveling screenwriter who reexamines his own life during a week spent hanging out with the cultural elite of 1920s Paris. The 2012 movie *Looper* is set in a version of 2044, in which assassins called "loopers" use time travel to target their victims. Their last victim is their future self.

In 1991, Diana Gabaldon wrote *Outlander*, the first book in a series about a twentieth-century nurse who is transported back into eighteenth-century Scotland by historic standing stones. The romance was turned into a TV series beginning in 2014.

So what comes next for time travel, both scientific and science fictional? Will scientists unlock the secrets of quantum entanglement and use exotic materials to stabilize a portal through a wormhole? Will the story of their triumphs inspire blockbuster books and movies? Only a time traveler to the future can know for sure.

1843 Charles Dickens's classic *A Christmas Carol* is published.

1889 Mark Twain's novel *A Connecticut Yankee in King Arthur's Court* is published.

1895 H. G. Wells's novel *The Time Machine* is published.

1905 Einstein's theory of special relativity is released.

1918 Einstein's theory of general relativity is released.

1927 Astrophysicist Arthur Eddington proposes that the "arrow of time" can only move forward.

1949 Kurt Gödel proposes a theoretical rotating universe that allows the possibility of time travel into the past.

1963 The first episode of the British TV program *Doctor Who* airs.

1969 Kurt Vonnegut's novel *Slaughterhouse-Five* is published.

1974 Frank Tipler proposes that time travel could be achieved by means of a huge rotating cylinder.

1980 Gregory Benford's novel *Timescape* is published.

1984 The movie *The Terminator* is released.

1985 Carl Sagan's novel *Contact* is published; the movie *Back to the Future* is released.

1988 Stephen Hawking describes concepts related to time and the universe to the general public in his popular nonfiction book *A Brief History of Time: From the Big Bang to Black Holes*.

1995 The movie *Twelve Monkeys* is released.

1999 Stephen Hawking delivers his lecture "Space and Time Warps."

2011 Stephen King's novel *11/22/63* is published.

2014 The movie *Interstellar* is released.

assassinate To commit a murder, often for political reasons.

black hole An object so dense that not even light can escape its gravity.

causal Involving a cause.

celestial Positioned in or relating to outer space.

conundrum A puzzling or difficult problem or question.

cosmology The study of the origin, evolution, structure, and eventual fate of the universe.

dimension An axis for geometric coordinates in space or time.

ethics A code of behavior that is considered correct or moral.

event A specific place and time in space-time.

field A region surrounding an object in which a force is exerted on other objects.

force A dynamic influence that causes a change in the motion of an object.

general relativity Einstein's 1915 theory explaining gravity as the curvature of space-time.

genre A category or class, especially in art or literature.

hard science fiction A type of science fiction that places scientific accuracy at the forefront.

hypothetical Pertaining to a proposed but unproven explanation that may be used to guide further investigation.

light-year The astronomical unit of distance equivalent to the distance that light travels in one year—about 5.88 trillion miles (9.46 trillion kilometers).

model A simplified representation of a system or phenomenon, such as in physics or computation, that may be used in the development of scientific theories.

paradox A statement or proposition that leads to a logically unacceptable conclusion even when based on sound premises.

portal An entrance such as a door or gate.

quantum physics The discipline of physics dealing with interactions of energy and matter on the subatomic scale.

satirical Using humor, sarcasm, or irony to criticize someone or something, often pertaining to current events.

scenario A projected or imagined sequence of events.

singularity A region in which the theories of mathematics and physics break down; for example, the center of a black hole.

space-time The four-dimensional system of coordinates including three physical dimensions combined with time.

special relativity Einstein's 1905 theory based on the principles that the laws of physics are the same for all inertial frames of reference and that the speed of light is constant.

speculative Based on conjecture rather than fact; hypothetical.

theoretical Concerned with ideas or conjecture rather than practical applications.

FOR MORE INFORMATION

American Institute of Physics (AIP)
One Physics Ellipse
College Park, MD 20740
(301) 209-3100
Website: http://www.aip.org
The AIP serves a federation of physical science societies in a common mission to promote physics and allied fields.

American Mathematical Society (AMS)
201 Charles Street
Providence, RI 02904-2294
(401) 455-4000
Website: http://www.ams.org
Facebook, Instagram, Twitter: @amermathsoc
The AMS, founded in 1888 to further the interests of mathematical research and scholarship, serves the national and international community through its publications, meetings, advocacy, and other programs.

Canada Science and Technology Museum
PO Box 9724, Station T
Ottawa, ON K1G 5A3
Canada
(866) 442-4416
Website: https://ingeniumcanada.org
Facebook and Twitter: @SciTechMuseum
The Canada Science and Technology Museum aims to help the public understand the ongoing relationships between science, technology, and Canadian society.

Canadian Association of Physicists (CAP)
555 King Edward Avenue, 3rd Floor
Ottawa, ON, K1N 7N5
Canada
(613) 562-5614
Website: http://www.cap.ca
Facebook: @CanadianAssociationOfPhysicists
Twitter: @CAPhys
CAP works to highlight achievements in Canadian physics and to pursue scientific, educational, public policy, and communication initiatives that enhance the vitality of the discipline.

Museum of Science Fiction
PO Box 88
Alexandria, VA 22313-0088
Website: http://www
 .museumofsciencefiction.org
Facebook:
 @museumofsciencefiction
Twitter: @ Museum_SciFi
The Museum of Science Fiction
 is in the process of opening a
 facility. Its mission is to provide displays of artifacts and
 interactive exhibits about
 science fiction and the history of the genre.

Physics World
IOP Publishing
Temple Circus
Temple Way
Bristol BS1 6HG
United Kingdom
+44 (0)117 929 7481
Website: http://
 physicsworld.com
Facebook: @physicsworld
Twitter: @PhysicsWorld
Physics World is the member maga-
 zine of the Institute of Physics
 (IOP), the society serving the
 global physics community.

Science Fiction and Fantasy Writ-
 ers of America (SFWA)
SFWA, Inc.
PO Box 3238
Enfield, CT 06083-3238
Website: http://www.sfwa.org
Facebook: @SFWA.org
Twitter: @SFWA
The SFWA is the organization for
 published authors, artists,
 and professionals working in
 fantasy and science fiction.

Space.com
150 Fifth Avenue, 9th Floor
New York, NY 10011
(212) 703-5800
Website: https://www.space.com
Facebook: @spacecom
Twitter: @SPACEdotcom
Space.com provides news on
 space exploration and astron-
 omy, including topics related
 to the nature of time, such as
 quantum physics and relativity.

FOR FURTHER READING

Alexander, Lloyd. *Time Cat: The Remarkable Journeys of Jason and Gareth.* New York, NY: Square Fish, 2012.

Binney, James. *Astrophysics: A Very Short Introduction.* New York, NY: Oxford University Press, 2016.

Blundell, Katherine M. *Black Holes: A Very Short Introduction.* New York, NY: Oxford University Press, 2015.

Hawking, Stephen. *The Illustrated A Brief History of Time. Updated and Expanded ed.* London, UK: Bantam Books, 2015.

Holzner, Steven. *Quantum Physics for Dummies.* Rev. ed. Hoboken, NJ: Wiley, 2013.

Jones, Diana Wynne. *A Tale of Time City.* New York, NY: Firebird, 2012.

L'Engle, Madeleine. *A Wrinkle in Time.* New York, NY: Square Fish, 2011.

Lightman, Alan. *Einstein's Dreams.* New York, NY: Vintage, 2004.

Stead, Rebecca. *When You Reach Me.* New York, NY: Wendy Lamb Books, 2009.

Whiting, Jim. *Space and Time.* Mankato, MN: Creative Education, 2014.

BIBLIOGRAPHY

Carroll, Sean. *From Eternity to Here: The Quest for the Ultimate Theory of Time.* New York, NY: Dutton, 2010.

Clegg, Brian. *How to Build a Time Machine: The Real Science of Time Travel.* New York, NY: St. Martin's Press, 2011.

Everett, Allen, and Thomas Roman. *Time Travel and Warp Drives: A Scientific Guide to Shortcuts Through Time and Space.* Chicago, IL: University of Chicago Press, 2012.

Gleick, James. *Time Travel: A History.* New York, NY: Pantheon Books, 2016.

Gott, Richard J. *Time Travel in Einstein's Universe: The Physical Possibilities of Travel Through Time.* Boston, MA: Houghton Mifflin Company, 2001.

Hawking, Stephen W., et al. *The Future of Spacetime.* New York, NY: W. W. Norton and Company, 2002.

Hawking, Stephen. "Space and Time Warps." 1999. Retrieved October 28, 2017. http://www.hawking.org.uk/space-and-time-warps.html.

Hunter, Joel. "Time Travel." Internet Encyclopedia of Philosophy. Retrieved September 25, 2017. http://www.iep.utm.edu/timetrav.

Jones, Matthew, and Joan Ormrod. *Time Travel in Popular Media: Essays on Film, Television, Literature and Video Games.* Jefferson, NC: McFarland and Company, Inc., 2015.

Kaplan, Sarah. "Quantum Entanglement, Science's 'Spookiest' Phenomenon, Achieved in Space." *Washington Post*, June 15, 2017. https://www.washingtonpost.com/news/speaking-of-science/wp/2017/06/15/quantum-entanglement-sciences-spookiest-phenomenon-achieved-in-space/.

Krauss, Lawrence M. *The Greatest Story Ever Told—So Far: Why Are We Here?* New York, NY: Atria Books, 2017.

Lockwood, Michael. *The Labyrinth of Time: Introducing the Universe.* New York, NY: Oxford University Press, 2005.

Randles, Jenny. *Breaking the Time Barrier: The Race to Build the First Time Machine.* New York, NY: Paraview Pocket Books, 2005.

"Researcher Uses Math to Investigate Possibility of Time Travel." Phys. org, April 27, 2017. https://phys.org/news/2017-04-math -possibility.html.

Smith, Nicholas J. J. "Time Travel." Stanford Encyclopedia of Philosophy, Spring 2016. https://plato.stanford.edu/archives/spr2016 /entries/time-travel.

Thorne, Kip. *The Science of Interstellar.* New York, NY: W. W. Norton and Company, 2014.

Toomey, David. *The New Time Travelers: A Journey to the Frontiers of Physics.* New York, NY: W. W. Norton and Company, 2007.

Wells, H. G. *The Time Machine.* New York, NY: Penguin Books, 2010.

Wolcholver, Natalie. "New Quantum Theory Could Explain the Flow of Time." *Wired*, April 25, 2014. https://www.wired.com /2014/04/quantum-theory-flow-time.

INDEX

A

Adams, Douglas, 15
Addington, Kate, 50
Amis, Martin, 44
Anderson, Poul, 35, 37
"arrow of time" argument, 43
Asimov, Isaac, 14

B

Back to the Future trilogy, 19, 21, 24
    and unethical time travel, 21, 26
Benford, Gregory, 15, 47
black holes, 33, 35
Borges, Jorge Luis, 13–14
Bradbury, Ray, 17, 24
*Brief History of Time: From the Big
    Bang to Black Holes, A* (Hawk-
    ing), 48–49
Butler, Octavia, 14–15
"By His Bootstraps" (Heinlein),
    24–25
    and multiple selves, 25

C

Chrichton, Michael, 21
Christmas Carol, A (Dickens), 7
Chu, Wesley, 47, 50
*Connecticut Yankee in King Arthur's
    Court, A* (Twain), 8
Contact (Sagan), 40

D

Dickens, Charles, 7
Doomsday Book (Willis), 17–18, 26

E

Eddington, Arthur, 43
Edge of Tomorrow, 22
Einstein, Albert, 28–31, 33
Einstein's Dreams (Lightman), 31
11/22/63 (King), 50
End of Eternity, The (Asimov), 14, 26
Everett, Hugh, 45, 47

F

Finney, Jack, 23
Forever War, The (Haldeman), 37
"forking path" theory of time, 14

G

Gabaldon, Diana, 52
"Garden of Forking Paths, The"
    (Borges), 13–14
Gödel, Kurt, 38, 40
"grandfather paradox," 24
Groundhog Day, 18

H

Haldeman, Joe, 37
Hawking, Stephen, 48–49
    and "Chronology Protection Con-
    jecture," 49
    and many-worlds theory, 49
Heinlein, Robert, 24–25
Hitchhiker's Guide to the Galaxy series
    (Adams), 15
*How to Live Safely in a Science Fic-
    tional Universe* (Chu), 47, 50
Hyperion (Simmons), 15

I

Interstellar, 41–42
Irving, Washington, 7

K

Kindred (Butler), 14–15
King, Stephen, 50

L

Life After Life (Addington), 50
Lightman, Alan, 31
Looper, 52

M

many-worlds theory, 45, 47
Marty McFly, 19, 24, 26
mass, as relative, 31
Massachusetts Institute of Technology (MIT), 4
Midnight in Paris, 52
"Mimsy Were the Borogroves" (Padgett), 22

N

Newton, Isaac, 27
Niffenegger, Audrey, 47

O

Outlander (Gabaldon), 52

P

Padgett, Lewis, 22
Planet of the Apes, 37

Primer, 50, 52

Q

quantum physics, 45, 47
and time travel, 45

R

Restaurant at the End of the Universe, The (Adams), 15
"Rip Van Winkle" (Irving), 7

S

Sagan, Carl, 40
Schwarzschild, Karl, 33
science, technology, engineering, and mathematics (STEM), 4–5
science fiction (literary genre), 4–5, 11, 13
"hard," 13
Simmons, Dan, 15
Slaughterhouse-Five (Vonnegut), 14
"Sound of Thunder, A" (Bradbury), 24, 26
space, as relative, 31
space-time continuum, 29–31
Spin (Wilson), 47
Stead, Rebecca, 50

T

Tau Zero (Anderson), 35, 37
and time dilation, 35, 37
Terminator, The, 21–22, 27
time
as absolute, 28

dilation, 31, 33, 35, 37
    as relative, 28–29, 31
    and speed of light, 30–31
    and string theory, 47
    and theory of general relativity, 33
    as unidirectional, 43
Time and Again (Finney), 23
Timecop, 27
Timeline (Chrichton), 21
Time Machine, The (Wells), 8–11,
        12–13
    impact on science fiction, 11, 13
    initial reaction to, 11
    objections to time travel ad-
        dressed, 11
time machines, 21–23
Time's Arrow (Amis), 44
Timescape (Benford), 15, 27, 47
time travel
    "butterfly effect," 24
    causal loop, 24–25
    in children's/young adult litera-
        ture, 15–16
    multiple selves, 25
    paradoxes, 24
    and quantum physics, 45
    as theoretically possible, 6
    vs. time slips, 22–23
Time Traveler, 9–11, 12, 13, 38
    as logical, 10
time traveler, origin of term, 8
Time Traveler's Wife, The (Niffeneg-
        ger), 47
Tipler, Frank, 40

Tipler cylinder, 40
"Toynbee Convector, The" (Brad-
        bury), 17
"Traversable Acausal Retrograde Do-
        main in Spacetime" (TARDIS;
        2017 paper), 6
Twain, Mark, 7
Twelve Monkeys, 27–28

V
Vonnegut, Kurt, 14

W
warp drives, 36–37
Wells, H. G., 8, 10–11, 12–13
    social issues and science fiction, 13
When You Reach Me (Stead), 50
Willis, Connie, 17–18
Wilson, Robert Charles, 47
wormholes, 36, 40

ABOUT THE AUTHOR

Corona Brezina is an author who has written numerous books for young adults. Several of her previous works have also focused on topics related to physics and the history of science, including *The Laws of Thermodynamics* and *The Scientist's Guide to Physics: Discovering Relativity*. She lives in Chicago, Illinois.

PHOTO CREDITS